GW01393187

JESUS
TEN QUESTIONS

JESUS
TEN QUESTIONS

DAVID STONE

BOURCHIER BOOKS

First published by Bourchier Books, an imprint of domtom publishing ltd, 2008.

ISBN 978-1-906070-08-3

Typesetting and Design by Glad Stockdale.

Printed & bound in the UK by DPS Partnership Ltd. www.dpsltd.net.

CONTENTS

THE STARTING POINT

I hope that the reader finds this book approachable, the sort of book that can be picked up when a moment offers, perhaps on train or plane or from a bedside table. It is not theology in the professional or technical sense; rather, it has grown from the jottings of a layman, a dilettante in divinity, sharing his thoughts and questions. There are no footnotes, no lists of source materials, nor any bibliography. There are no cross-references within the book itself, though there are threads common to all the discussions. Some of it, I admit, may read rather like a Zip file, with the occasional sentence temptingly calling to be 'unpacked'. But if there are layers of meaning, the reader will be the explorer if he or she wants — which is a courteous, modern way of saying 'who hath ears to hear, let him hear'.

It attempts to offer a way of thinking about Jesus, his motivation, mission and image, understood from a viewpoint that communicates in the light of today's knowledge and attitudes, untrammelled by the interpretations, stumbling-blocks and misunderstandings of our own invention over the centuries, history's accumulated paraphernalia. Giuseppe di Lampedusa wrote of Graham Greene that 'he has gone back to the roots of Christianity and has cleansed it of all the cardinals, the Luthers, the archbishops of Canterbury, the Madonnas of Syracuse, the Puritans and the Jesuits and he has found its true face, the face of charity'. It is along that way my thoughts lead me, and more. What actually impelled Jesus?

There are several fine and lucid books that lay out the necessary detailed research, fertile soil for answers; and any curiosity the reader may come to feel about the facts behind these jottings, any need for justification, may be served by these. I owe a great deal to the books mentioned on page 72. But even were I academically qualified to follow the scholarly path to the truth, I would not here want to run the risk of indulging in what could become a dangerously satisfying diversion and challenge. All my observations are based on, or can be found in, the Gospels, and Paul's Letters; but I did not want these essays to be any sort of exegesis or, as it were, a sermon. If a reader has any comments or queries, the best place to go for elucidation is the New Testament. As for the philosophical, mystical or spiritual content, I hardly think that there is anything new here: in one way or another the ideas have been about for centuries. However, I have generally resisted any temptation to name those writers, great authorities, who through the ages have explored the thoughts that follow. It is the substance that counts, not its mediators.

The fashion of trying to find out and state in overt specific and historical terms who and what Jesus really was can be dated roughly from the eighteenth century, though the question itself has always existed in some form, even in his own lifetime. The efforts have ranged from questioning whether he ever existed, to attempts to establish an almost daily diary of his movements and sayings, to the complex and meticulous literary analyses of the Gospel writings initiated by German scholars in the nineteenth century in an effort to relegate discrepancies and produce an Ur-text Gospel, one 'original' document, probably in Greek. The tools of textual criticism, comparison of manuscripts, literary style and vocabulary, have been both valuable and revelatory in producing an understanding of increasing integrity. But at the same time, these analyses have in effect also tended to produce diversity and veil the essential message.

Today the scene is continually changing: some previous conclusions are being developed or discarded, thanks to the new discoveries of the past century and the present scientific advances in dating and other analytical methods, archaeological research, newly found old documents and the modern ability to collate all such findings quickly. The scene will continue to change: the detective story continues. But Oscar Wilde's comment 'the English are always degrading truths into facts' has an application way beyond the national.

Jesus was motivated by an overwhelming impulse to discover, create and communicate a revelation. Mozart, in his medium of music, was compelled to produce harmonies, structures, phrases that communicate by satisfying our emotional and instinctive recognition of their total rightness; examples abound in all walks of life and human endeavour. Jesus, in his medium of the human condition, communicates in the same way. Theology, the study of what for want of a more precise word is generally called God, embraces science, religion, philosophy, literary analysis, medicine, archaeology, mystical inspiration, psychiatry and more. You do not have to be a believer to be a theologian. As a subject its fascination can be compelling and the implications endless, and there can come moments of untrammelled recognition that you have met something essentially right. Just as in music a modulation, a single chord, a thematic recapitulation has an indefinable power to penetrate the listener's heart, acknowledged by all; so, in theology as in other arts and sciences, these moments of instinctive recognition of the truth occur. Once recognized and harnessed, this awareness could contribute to a new age for which many men and women may now be looking: that is, the establishment of some shared spiritual standpoint and inner objective. In his 1970 Nobel Speech on Literature, 'One Word of Truth', Alexander Solzhenitsyn said 'the genuinely artistic work is utterly, irrefutably convincing' and 'a work of art carries its proof in itself'. I have come to understand that the life, teaching and personality of the man called Jesus reveals him as the greatest artist of all.

I have tried to be objective. Yet the initial response of those who came in contact with Jesus in his own time was an emotional one, positive or negative. Even the awesome intellect of Paul was emotionally triggered. This instant, instinctive communication is rare today. There is a need to find some way of looking at Jesus that reopens this contact, just as we respond to the same power in great art. So much stands in the way: the difference between our own awareness today and the knowledge and way of life of his contemporaries, men's attempts over the centuries to make him a reflection of our own thoughts and abilities, the abuses of his message, distorted for our own purposes. But if there is anywhere in these pages a grain of food for thought, according to each reader's own needs and nature, something may be set in motion.

And so the following questions are used as springboards for comment. They are put very directly. Even fifty years ago there were many who would have been shocked to hear these questions so openly and rashly asked. And today there may be those Christians who will find them objectionable, irrelevant, pitiable; or, more seriously, upsetting and destructive of valuable and cherished beliefs. But it was Jesus himself who reputedly said 'there are many mansions in my Father's house'. The implication is that in heaven every individual's character has a place, lasting and permanent (the Greek used means 'durable') – providing there is belief. It has not been my intention to encourage a watered-down, hazy interpretation of Jesus; or to challenge the function of any Church's accepted dogma; or to massage Jesus' image so as to be comfortably accepted by all and sundry. If such seems the effect of my thoughts, I shall have an immense load of blame to carry.

Finally, I have to comment on the use of certain words. Today one of the biggest stumbling-blocks to approaching and understanding Jesus is the word God. It has come to carry immediate anthropomorphic connotations and images. The Book of Genesis states that God created man in his own image: it is a truism to say that man has actually created God in man's own image, attempting to elevate himself to the immortal divine. The power that impelled Jesus in his search and subsequent teaching and actions has been given many names: God, the Holy Spirit, the Logos, the Word, among many. I have to use these terms to save laborious and time-wasting definitions and circumlocutions. This may well be a limiting factor, since for many readers such terms may already be a turn-off. But how else can one speak of the primal power?

*   *   *

For quotations from the Bible I have used both the Authorized Version and the New English Bible. In order to avoid repetitive qualifications I have used the singular word Church to mean the organized community or communities who in various ways and degrees profess a belief in Jesus Christ and accept Christianity as their stated religion.

1

WHO KILLED JESUS?

Jesus was executed by the overall authority then ruling Judaea, the Romans. It was, however, in part at the instigation of the indigenous Judaean civil administration, specifically elements of today what one might term the Establishment. How far the latter were involved must always remain a moot point, since the Gospels were written partly from the anti-Jewish standpoint that grew up in the generations after Jesus' death: the very specific accounts of the involvement of Sanhedrin members and the Chief Priest would easily be elaborated in these circumstances – people have a strong tendency to enjoy blaming and to point the finger. With the prevailing atmosphere of a country with a very strong nationalist movement and what almost amounted to an army of occupation, any popular manifestation, any focus of emotional excitement in the context of the country's religion was of concern to the Roman authority. But the story is not about Romans and Jews: who were the protagonists is irrelevant.

It is about human nature. The phenomenon is not specific to any culture or age: we have witnessed recently some of the same forces at work in the death of David Kelly and in the moral cowardice of the BBC's ensuing response. The fatal outcome of Jesus' ministry was as inevitable as the final act of a Greek tragedy, given the circumstances of the political environment and human nature.

These elements conspired together, the Roman and the Judaean, both at administrative level. For the Romans there were political expedience, some nervousness, and a perceived necessity to act at a specific time – the annual celebration of the Passover at Jerusalem, when the crowds had gathered and religious sensitivity was high – with a continuing show of strength. For the Jewish civil Establishment, understandable jealousy, self-protection and self-interest worked with the more positive acceptance of responsibility in an effort to control the unruly elements of their own countrymen and to avoid the sort of Roman backlash that was to destroy Jerusalem and the Temple in AD 70 – when, significantly, the Romans replaced the priests as Jewish leaders with the rabbis. This need to control the populace was motivated by fear of what could result from the possible political influence of Jesus; by a general need to assert authority during an explosive period; and the more unseemly motivation of every Establishment to contain perceived dissidents and to retain authority. Such fears were not surprising when one takes into account that Judas Iscariot was a member of one of the nationalist freedom movements (in passing, it is a sidelight to find Jesus' great-nephews in the list of revolutionary leaders at the time of the Emperor Domitian, as recorded by Eusebius); Jesus' disciples were representative and chosen for a purpose.

Amongst some of his fellow countrymen, too, there may perhaps have been some confused thinking, or a failure to think at all, in not recognizing the difference between Jesus' spiritual message and the earthly slogans of the nationalist movement: in other words, that a saviour of Israel, a messiah, did not have to be a political saviour. Jesus was indeed, in modern parlance, a power-monger, but the power was not what our modern word implies. A moral attitude can be used to justify self-seeking survival: China's rulers borrowed western, communist socialism, the ANC in South Africa latched onto the western belief that apartheid was evil but practised forms of apartheid in their own communities. Jesus had no axe of survival to grind: survival was unimportant to him. He refused to start or head a party. He essentially addressed the soul of the individual. How easy it is for such an attitude to get annoyingly under the skin of any ardently committed political such as Judas.

With all this, and the age-old need for the Establishment, even if composed of political forces usually in conflict, to hang together – blinded by anxieties and knowledge of what mass hysteria can do, thinking in the short term, unable to see where their actions would lead, how could they help themselves? – the end was already written.

There was nothing blasphemous in being hailed as a messiah. A messiah is not God: throughout history messiahs have been accepted and recognized as men sent by God to save a nation. One of the most recent examples was the Mahdi in Sudan, just the sort of leader, initially religious and latterly political, whom the Jewish authorities knew would bring about severe Roman reaction. It was not an actual contravention of the Jewish faith that led to Jesus' death. Given parallel political circumstances it could have happened in any country and in any century.

These then were the worldly triggers of his death. Did Jesus use them deliberately to bring about his death because he saw himself as a sacrifice, an atonement for human sin? A belief in Jesus' death and resurrection is a manifestation of the indomitably optimistic spirit that is innate in man, the desire for good to triumph over evil, the resolve not to accept death as our finite end. To believe Jesus' death was an atonement is a recognition of the reality of sin, an awareness of a barrier between us and God, an expression of the need to be reassured that there is a means to break through the veil. How far this sort of thinking, conscious or unconscious, is part of today's attitudes is a moot point. The concept of sacrifice was certainly part of life in Jesus' day, an instinctive acknowledgement of our failings, our mortal nature and the hope that there is a power beyond us. It had been ingrained from the beginning of mankind and been developed into a concrete system that in its purest form offered a way to approach and associate with God: its most distorted form can be expressed by 'I want to buy some religion: how much will it cost me?' The true doctrine of sacrifice is not readily to hand to many, possibly most, modern people, though the doctrine of atonement is very much at the heart of the Christian faith. The extent to which it formed a conscious motivation in Jesus' thought, and, if it did, for how long before his death, can only remain questions: it is useless to think one can define with certainty what Jesus himself actually thought, in this matter as in any other. It was definitely after Jesus' ministry that Jesus was acknowledged and understood as a sacrifice in the sense of the traditional Passover lamb.

It appears likely that Jesus spoke of his approaching death only in the final period of his life. Matthew's account is an exception; but its author seemed to have a line of special pleading about the Old Testament. John speaks quite early of a plan to kill Jesus, but he puts no precise words about this into Jesus' mouth at any stage. Luke's qualifying remarks show him to be uncomfortable in ascribing any detailed forecast to an earlier period. From the reactions at the time it seems that the bewildered and shattered disciples could have had no firm forecast, no accepted preparation, to soften their bewilderment when it happened. Jesus seems never to have reinforced his intimations with exact quotations from the prophets, and none of his parables speaks of the Cross. The idea that he consciously planned his actions, including his own death, to fit a selection of writings in the Old Testament is to ascribe a sort of casuistry to him. Yet Jesus' total immersion in Jewish religious writings had led him to the sort of insight and revelation that belongs to genius: they were an integral part of him, and in fact his whole life became, by instinct, a parable. It was only after the event that the writers of the Gospels turned to the strategy of scriptural vindication with the phrase 'according to the Scriptures', to qualify what at the time must have seemed a catastrophe.

One can, however, readily identify with the New Testament writers, the thinkers among the early followers of Jesus. On reflection, Jesus' life and teaching tied in with, and gave the clue to, a significant amount of the Old Testament; and the events of his life could even be symbolically identified with certain of the Jewish annual rituals, as the author of John's Gospel shows (even to the extent of probably changing the timeline facts). There is a thread. One can hear them say, with enthusiasm and wonder, 'so Jesus is what it is all about'.

There is a corollary to linking Jesus' death to forecast prophesies. Some will ask the question 'did God kill Jesus?' The idea that his death was part of God's universal plan carries so many imposed layers of anthropomorphic connotations, so much arrogance given the limitations of man's thinking, that to consider it would call for an approach of the utmost circumspection, and an endless exegesis. Again, a narrow interpretation of a word, prophesy, clouds the issue. The so-called prophets were feeling their way to the nature of God: they were not Nostradamus.

If then we accept the need for an atonement – in its fundamental sense of finding a way of blotting out our human failings in order to be at one with God – it was Jesus' life and example that was the atonement. This concept of atonement does not equate with the negative idea of Jesus sacrificially offered as a necessary intermediary in the sense of standing between us and God: limitation, denial of entry to God's presence, was counter to his nature. Thus, by believing in the spirit that he, a man, manifested and by aligning ourselves with it, we can approach what is generally called God, we can in our times and each according to his nature apply the primal power to the environment of our own human condition. In this sense Jesus offers a way to union with God: Jesus is the nearest man will get to God.

There is yet one more aspect to Jesus' death, and that the most important. He died because he loved us. He had to hold to his purpose of revealing the truth to us, come what may, without compromise, even when it became clear where it would lead. And his message lives on, unvanquished, indeed empowered, by his death.

2

DID JESUS EXIST?

Yes. Quite apart from the non-Christian documentary references, it is inconceivable that his actions, teaching and character could have been created by someone, like some master novel of all novels which was then taken as a text for reinterpretation in various ways by the Gospels. To create a fictional character and a story to match that character was not in line with the way first-century authors thought and worked. And yet the Gospels, compilations of written lists of sayings, oral and eyewitness accounts, interspersed with the authors' interpretations and influenced by their evangelical purpose, are unique both in the first century and for a long time afterwards in terms of literary content and style. None of the authors sets out to describe Jesus: nowhere is there a portrait of him or his character. Yet the shadowed picture of the man Jesus is remarkably consistent.

He has insight and perception; he understands the various people with whom he has dealings on a one-to-one basis; he employs ambiguities to good purpose and displays psychological adroitness; he speaks specifically to the needs of single individuals – sometimes in terms of that person only, sometimes in terms that have come to enjoy general application through the ages; he employs the parable style of teaching common in his day, but with a unique skill and quality. Jesus' parables have an awareness and grasp of reality in every word and action; every line carries a meaning – they are extraordinarily vivid and succinct, indeed so involving that not only the Gospel writers but monks through the centuries, as they copied his words, were tempted to interpret and comment, sure proofs of the power of his communication and direct contact.

He always grasps the essence of a situation; he admits ignorance; his lifestyle is not necessarily stern, although to some of his contemporaries, even to his family at the start, he may have appeared way-out. But he is not a crank; he does not subsist on locusts and wild honey or wear a hairshirt. He enjoys a good meal; he associates with 'sinners'. He has the strongest grasp of reality and lives in the day-to-day world. He displays tension at times; he can be angry, short-tempered, sharp-tongued, yet compassionate and generous. He accepts the need to get away from his family. He has studied the psalms, the prophets and all the Jewish biblical writings to such a depth that they have become integral to his inherent thinking – there is no conscious effort in his use of them. The use of 'truly I say to you', a phrase not found elsewhere, is habitual.

His insistence on the true meaning of religion without the man-dominated ritual of formal sacrifice aroused frustration and sudden anger in the incident with the traders in the Temple. His heartbreaking disappointment is evident in the tears shed for Jerusalem's failure to understand the prophets, and in his apparent cursing of the fig tree that bore no fruit (the prophet Micah describes Israel's failure as a barren fig tree).

And let us not lose touch with reality: as he hangs on the cross his words 'My God, why have you forsaken me?' – a direct quotation from the Jewish psalms – is the natural cry of desolation from a man undergoing excruciating pain, total exhaustion, dehydration and delirium, whatever the theologians may wish to make of them.

One consistent personality emerges from the record of all the New Testament writings. In spite of the multiple authors involved and whatever the inconsistencies of time, place and detail, this is such a personality as could only be created by a single great author today: and even then it would be without the genuine immediacy and clarity that only a real person generates and that permeates the Gospels.

In defining this man the question 'did Jesus seek poverty?' must sooner or later be asked. To seek and practise poverty has always been a mark of the so-called spiritual life, according to many religions. Jesus was willing to sacrifice material comfort when necessary; but he did not make a point of shunning the good things of life when they were offered him. Nor were his disciples chosen specifically because they were poor men: by no means were all poor. Just for one instance we know that Peter and Andrew may well have had their own business with a large (eight-metre) boat or boats and crew employees. His followers came from all strata of society. And Jesus' command to the rich young man to sell everything and follow him was surely an assessment of that particular person's needs, character and capability, rather than the declaration of a generalized rule or a rejection of those who were not poor.

It was for him a question of what was the primary focus of one's actions and thoughts. A disciplined pursuit of poverty and a rejection of the enjoyment of life as a means of earning brownie points, both in the eyes of one's associates and as an insurance policy for the future life, would have appeared very wrong to him, selfish to a degree. If such a way of thinking were applied to the use of ritual and sacrifice as a way of currying favour with God, he would actually attack. The father embraces his prodigal son with love, and makes no demands. The master forgives the unjust steward because 'you told the truth'. There, in a nutshell, is the opposition between ritual and regulations on the one hand, and individual instinct and conscience on the other. Throughout Jesus' words there is this acknowledgement that there exists a more potent force than ethics – the absolute, innate recognition of God's spirit. Yet to make some outward gesture as a sign of gratitude and thanks was a different matter, to be encouraged, since thanksgiving is joyous and positive. To take life as it comes while refusing to pursue wealth as an end in itself is one way of accepting a power beyond oneself. To pursue poverty as a way of claiming merit is false. Whatever our achievement may be, to claim merit is to limit the bounds of achievement, to be an unprofitable servant.

The real challenge does not lie in deciding whether Jesus existed or not. It lies in understanding Jesus in the light of the thought processes, the beliefs and the political scenarios and the politics of his day, reaching a degree of identification and then adapting it to our contemporary lives.

3

ARE JESUS' LIFE AND TEACHING ACCURATELY RECORDED BY THE GOSPELS?

The Gospels defy classification. They are an amalgamation of reportage, received fact, allegories, parables, symbols and symbolic events, surmise, self-expression, proselytizing, comment, teaching. They are written by men – that is to say, people with individual attitudes, different and specific audiences in mind, different skills and talents, varying attitudes and purposes.

And the challenge is rather like the question 'what is authenticity?' posed by the Early Music Movement. In musical performance today we can use all the tools of, say, the eighteenth century, we can benefit from the research into the styles of the period as recorded by written texts, and we can attempt to reproduce performance as of the eighteenth century. But we cannot play as they did, we cannot listen like an eighteenth-century audience, because we are not eighteenth-century people. To get inside the Gospels we really need to be first-century people. The writers were not constrained by today's insistence on proven and researched facts. They were concerned with one primary purpose, to communicate and portray the spiritual truth and meaning of the man Jesus. They were imbued with religious enthusiasm. They believed in their mission, aroused in the first place by an emotional response. The intellectual development of theology as a clinical study comes later.

Mark's Gospel is the nearest to an uninfluenced, unbiased record, but certainly not according to the techniques we employ today for the research and analysis of evidence. All the Gospels proclaim a message: some teach and explain more than Mark. Matthew's writer tries to get the message over from several viewpoints, particularly of those who had been expecting the arrival of the Old Testament messiah; and he tends to over-interpret. Luke offers an introduction that gives an impression of historically accurate placing: research shows that it is not accurate. But Luke did not have our resources to hand, and even we ourselves are not always clear as to the dating of events in our own lives.

To describe spiritual revelation in words is very difficult; but the writer of John, clearly after deep and long meditation, does his best. He explains to us much of what Jesus really meant by employing direct speech on Jesus' behalf, putting words in Jesus' mouth which seem to be interpretations – though, again, some may be original Jesus. He understands what the prophets were struggling to express and tells us in his own way that this was embodied in human form. He even seems to have fitted the narrative order of events to reinforce his own message that Jesus fulfilled the Jewish Law as the answer to generations of expectancy and searching. His understanding of the Second Coming is spiritual.

Although John's Gospel gives hints at times of the author's being an eyewitness to some events, generally the Gospel writers were dependent upon oral tradition, stories that were circulating and had been handed down across a generation or two, stories that were chosen and prioritized in order to meet the different challenges experienced by the early Christians from their different backgrounds and attitudes, Jewish, Roman and Greek. There were no stenographers on hand to be Jesus' Boswell. The criteria for the inclusion of a saying or an event were not the criteria likely to be employed today. Could it serve the writers' purposes? Would it fit, or be made to fit, their beliefs? To what part of the narrative could it best be allocated? The Gospels were hung together on a skeleton of a remembered timeframe: they reflect the accumulated traditions of up to perhaps 110 years after Jesus came to be thought of as God.

The authors must also have been influenced, however indirectly, by Paul's teachings, and also by the then current concepts of other religious thinkers, such as the communities that we now know produced and used the Dead Sea Scrolls, some of which were written during Jesus' lifetime. Over the years interpretations of Jesus' sayings became part of the sayings themselves: this also applies to the comments of the later *scriptores*, the monks copying the texts. In other words, the Gospels show us what the writers thought of Jesus and what he meant to them and to their communities. The writers all demonstrate total faith. The Gospels are men's inspired attempts to share their knowledge and belief in their overwhelmingly certain experience of what infuses life, using practical imagery and examples.

The word 'faith' prompts a mention of two damaging misunderstandings. Comment is called for about an attitude loosely associated with so-called fundamentalism. A mountain range of confusion, distraction and misunderstanding has been raised between us and the meaning of biblical writings by a simple mistranslation of the Greek word 'Logos'. The Bible in English translates this as 'the Word'. The whole Bible is indeed a book that records and seeks to reveal the Logos, but Logos as the primary energy, the Law of all life. The actual words of the Bible are not wholly literal fact. It is a human narrative of events, didactic stories, the interpretation of the thoughts of the writers and allegories. It uses every means possible to attempt to reveal the nature of this primal energy called God, according to the knowledge, the understanding and the mores of the various periods and circumstances in which the authors lived. To love God is more important than belief, as an article of faith, that everything written in the Bible is fact.

Also, the meaning of the word 'faith' has been distorted by the accretion of a secondary meaning, credulousness. This is not a necessity in order to be accepted into the Christian community. True faith, on the contrary, is a blind understanding (Paul's conversion experience was blinding) where the emphasis is on understanding. Acceptance – faith – unlocks understanding. Belief has to be childlike, impervious to the thick tangle of men's intellectual gyrations accumulated around and over the pure spring.

There are illogical and contradictory strands and statements in all Gospels; and sometimes a confusion in understanding aspects of Jesus and his teaching. But in spite of the contradictions, the discrepancies of fact and timeline and the different emphases put on Jesus' teachings, the Gospels are a revelation of one message. The spirit of Jesus' teaching is unadulterated. It speaks through the Gospels easily and directly to us, just as Jesus did to each of his listeners. There is an honesty, an integrity that is irrefutable. This is the measure of its truth.

4

DID JESUS PERFORM MIRACLES?

The ambience of our day-to-day lives now, our way of thought, our awareness, the tools for the jobs we do, are delineated by the scientific discoveries and their applications that have escalated to a flood over, say, the last three centuries, a flood ever increasing. The line has hardened between what we today call reality, things we see and tangibly experience, and the ill-defined emotions and clouds of the mind, things of the spirit, mysticism. Our approach so often asks 'is this or that fact or fiction?' The edges of imagination have been blunted, or even destroyed, by the cut-and-dried, the black-and-white character of those knowledge and communication machines, the Web and the mobile SMS screen, with their inescapably automated responses. Wonder and awe are today limited to space exploration or black holes, and even these are becoming rapidly accepted without thought or appreciation.

This was not the case in Jesus' day. The difference in mental attitude and perception of our world is such that were we to be transported, like Mark Twain's Yank in the Court of King Arthur, to first-century Judaea, we would be fazed. Its terms of reference for living would be unknown to us; the people of the day were motivated by very different attitudes and sorts of knowledge, or lack of knowledge. It is well nigh impossible to put oneself into the mind of a first-century writer. For a few sentences or paragraphs the world we encountered would go along reasonably familiarly; and then we would walk straight into a brick wall.

So often today do Blake's words apply: 'The tree which moves some to tears of joy is in the eyes of others only a green thing which stands in the way.' This understanding has been demonstrated repeatedly in the visual arts, for example, by Munch's *Sun* mural in Oslo University. Indeed, to measure oneself against the way one appreciates the physical universe has always been one of the windows on to the meaning of God.

We have seen that the Gospels are an amalgamation of many categories of writing, reportage, allegories, parables, comment and so on. The transition between these is sometimes blurred; often there is no transition; and a single passage can explore several layers of application. So it is with the recorded miracles. Questions arise when some of them are subjected to the material, down-to-earth, factual approach of today. But are these accounts put forward as facts? Are they intended as allegories or parables to express spiritual truths? Would first-century readers have made such a difference? Their value and inner significance, that is, the reason they are recorded, exist of themselves and cannot be invalidated by a mistaken and inapplicable approach. Admittedly, to a first-century non-Christian audience, they would well be credible as literal truth; and it would have been a natural transition to turn remarkable acts of healing into the category of miracles, that is, the use of supernatural powers by a god. Today, to believe every one of the records of so-called miracles to be literal truth is to misunderstand them fundamentally; to dismiss them as superstitious efforts to bolster Jesus as a supernatural power is to throw out the baby with the bathwater.

Like the Kingdom of God motif, they are yet another way of explaining to us, in as compelling a way as possible, that there is a primal power – call it God if you like – that heals, that calls forth life, that permeates the physical world, and that Jesus was active evidence of it. The miracles, the Kingdom of God motif, the parables, his own actions, the events of his life and death, all these spell out the integrity of the single message put in so many ways, thanks to Jesus' intellectual grasp of all the tools he used to communicate.

These essays are not about definitions: the spirit we are discussing remains indefinable. We all know roughly what we mean by a miracle, and we know the subjects of the so-called miracle reports in the New Testament – healing, returning the dead to life, controlling the elements, feeding the multitude. But it is misleading to consider the so-called miracles as one entity. Some are descriptions of events, some carry metaphorical or allegorical messages, some are useful teaching aids.

The miracles of healing, mental and physical, appear to be factual record. There were in Jesus' day several holy men and miracle workers with such healing capabilities. It may well be that access to some form of primal energy, today

ascribed to alternative therapies, and as yet undiscovered
or undefined by science, was more readily and generally
achieved in the first century than in the modern world.
The accounts are credible much as they stand, given the
influence, authority and power of the spirit animating
Jesus. They are motivated by his compassion, not by any
intention of proving his credentials.

The feeding of the five thousand and/or four thousand
may have an origin in an event of some kind, even if
we accept that they are variant repetitions of the Old
Testament story of Elisha's feeding one hundred men with
twenty loaves. Here we move towards the allegory: if you
have faith, the spirit of God provides a rich feast of more
than enough; and, a less immediate interpretation but
nevertheless valid, one's own resources are inexhaustible if
you are aligned with God. The raising of Lazarus and the
daughter of Jairus from death (or, in the girl's case, where
the accounts actually differ, from a coma), again appear to
be factual, as well as allegorically illustrating Jesus' life-
giving force. Jesus' walking on water and stilling the storm
are typical legends demonstrating the truth that there is no
escape from danger without faith and also that the universe
is one interacting entity motivated by God.

But all the miracle stories admit, in varying degree, of
spiritually symbolic interpretation, and all these events
are part of Jesus' message about the Kingdom of God.
Again and again he uses real, practical acts as images, as
symbols of his meaning. This is one of many reasons for the
immediacy, the power of his communication technique and

its enduring quality. He found a shared point of contact with his audience; but they could read into these so-called miracles as much or as little as they chose or were capable of reading. The image penetrates their minds and, through conscious or unconscious digestion, bears fruit. An exegesis of each miracle story is not called for here, tempting though it may be to indulge one's mind and imagination. Suffice to say that the miracles are an incidental outcome of the primal spirit's irresistible presence in Jesus. With Jesus dedicated to and accepting such a creative, positive force, contact with him could have astounding effect.

5

WAS JESUS CONCEIVED BY A VIRGIN?

What is to be made of this part of Jesus' nativity story? The only mention of a virgin birth throughout the whole New Testament is in the Christmas narrative of Luke's and Matthew's opening chapters. It seems to have been unknown to Mark and John, as well as to Paul: it is hardly possible that the tradition of such an unusual phenomenon was so well known to these writers that they took it for granted. We know that other legends about Mary and Jesus' birth were current in the first century, and the suggestion has been made that this one was to be found in certain geographic areas but not everywhere. There is also some significance in what we now know to have been errors of fact in Luke's nativity story, as may be expected of an account taken down from stories circulating orally a generation or three after the events, and given the difference between the attitude at the time and ours as to historical accuracy. But certainly the writers of Luke and Matthew believed Mary to have been a virgin when Jesus was born, even if Luke then seems to offer an alternative in describing Jesus to be of Joseph's bloodline.

Yet again, it is a matter of reviewing the accounts from the contemporary standpoint: to apply modern scientific knowledge renders the legend impossible.

Was there a reason for its inclusion in these two Gospels? Several theories can be suggested. Matthew's author links it to an Old Testament prophecy; but he has to massage and mistranslate the prophesy to make it fit, and the prophesy is clearly used to add authority to an existing story. It is not an invention to fulfil a prophesy. The story carries the affirmation that God is at work; but, thirty years or more after the recognition of what he was about, Jesus does not need a virgin birth to give him credence and authority. Nor is it necessary to build whole theological structures around the question of Jesus' apparent supernatural status, as based primarily on this story, in order to experience the joy of Jesus' message. Perhaps there is a debt to contemporary Hellenic culture, which then embraced several myths of birth through divine parthenogenesis; these may have accounted for the development of the tradition by association. Thus, the authority of Jesus could only belong to a god; a god who actually appeared on earth in material form would almost certainly have an immortal as one parent.

The story may also be an allegorical, unconscious effort to express the fundamental truth, dimly perceived by the early believers, that Jesus embodied the essential creative force; but that does not make it necessary for him to have a supernatural birth. That Jesus was not conceived, that is, not born in the accepted sense, carries the implication that he lives eternally – without birth there cannot be death: the idea paves the way for the Resurrection. But so complex a mental speculation has no bearing on Jesus' message and is foreign to the writers of Matthew and Luke. We enter very deep waters if we relate the virgin birth to the doctrine that Jesus was sinless and, accordingly, free from human failings: the idea negates one of the significances of his being crucified, amongst many other implications that have caused trouble over the centuries.

The real challenge for today's churchgoers comes in the Church's Nicene Creed with its implied ritual insistence on, or confirmation of, belief in the virgin birth as a condition of acceptance into the Church, and thus material for a test of faith.

Let us be realistic. Once heard, the story just had to be included. It is one of the greatest, and simplest, expressions of joy and love we have. The singing stars, the animals, the symbolic riches of the Wise Men, Mary's quietness, the poor warmth and homeliness of the stable, Joseph's love, are all blended and focused in the child, an indescribably emotive combination, full of meaning.

Included it was. The result has been far reaching, especially in the elevation of Mary to be a cult figure. This is not the place to describe the need for such a figure or the use which later expanding Christianity made of Mary to replace the pagan female goddesses. Nor does this discussion in any way belittle the stature and nature of Mary or the effect she has had as an icon of tenderness, common sense, love, steadfastness and motherliness. One of Christianity's achievements – it is ongoing – has been

to elevate and recognize the status of women. In this the
figure of Mary has played a crucial role; but, even more so,
Jesus himself.

Jesus' attitude to women, in terms of first-century
Judaism, defied convention. Women were regarded as
second-class citizens. To converse with a woman outside
the family circle was hardly the thing; yet time and again
he spoke with them directly, sometimes in very perceptive
depth. He upheld the Law in his advice to them, but did not
shrink from risking the traditional accusation of spiritual
impurity through associating even with loose women.
In this situation he made his position very clear to his
followers and the attendant crowd, in his turn challenging
us all with the true spirit of mercy, understanding and
generosity. A corollary of his attitude towards women is his
antipathy at most times to natural male aggression, even
if he himself was capable of a sharp word or attacking the
Temple dealers. It says much for women that the Gospel
accounts record their presence with him as he died, their
ministrations to his corpse, their discovery of the empty
tomb, their meeting with the resurrected Christ, at the
same time as they record his desertion by most of if not all
his male followers.

Rabbis were then allowed and indeed encouraged
to marry, as they are today. But there is no evidence of
marriage, no mention of a wife for Jesus. This is hardly to
be wondered at: his sense of urgency, his total commitment
to his mission, his concentration explain this, as many great
creative artists have found. And seen thus, it becomes less a

matter of conscious self-abnegation and more an indication of a dedication that results in self-abnegation.

Is the concept of a virgin birth of crucial importance? Can we not share in the spirit that inspired Jesus, can we not align ourselves with the Logos, can we not live fully, can we not join in the Kingdom of God unless we are convinced that Jesus was conceived by a virgin? What is the relevance to the truth, the way and the life that Jesus offers? None. Jesus asked for belief in himself, that is, the message he proclaimed and the spirit he manifested. The absence of a virgin birth cannot invalidate Jesus' revelation.

6

DID JESUS CREATE CHRISTIANITY?

Jesus was concerned with motivation, attitude and action, not dogma. A complex religion about Jesus is not the same as the uncomplicated religion of Jesus. The discussions and debates of the Church, today and over the centuries, necessary or unnecessary, have little influence on the challenge at the coalface of human life of aligning oneself with the force that we call God.

But Jesus' teaching and story have survived. If, for argument's sake, we put aside the truths he embodied and their relevance for the human condition, history could have registered him as just another holy man; in his day preachers and holy men were a dime a dozen. Any good manager knows that, because of human failings, any initiative, any project, has to be given a structure to survive and succeed. And this is what Paul's supreme intellect, theological genius and instinctive emotional commitment helped to create. There is endless material to be mined out of Jesus by human intellect, to be shaped and developed to form structures and systems; much of Christian dogma is latent in Jesus' teaching. To put over spiritual ideas in words is difficult. Jesus used both words, often very concretely descriptive examples, and actions: indeed, the very events of his life add up to a parable. In doing so, he provided plenty of material for theologians to enlarge on over centuries: Paul extrapolated a pattern from what he knew of Jesus, but the pattern was there to be extrapolated. The risk lay in not obscuring Jesus' flame. Even James hints at Paul's confusing efforts. Paul is striving, in part, to define and show us an order, a system, by which to measure ourselves, a compass to lead us to a better condition and a support in reshaping any ignorance or bewilderment on our part – that is, if we find we are ignorant and bewildered. Through the centuries the ongoing interpretation of Jesus has been formulated in theological terms; this started almost immediately after his death.

To be positive, the Christian faith, in its rituals, hierarchies, dogma and codifications gives one expression to Jesus' teaching and life in a practical and tangible form that can be used and grasped by us, a sort of map: this has led to and sustained some of the most selfless acts of true purity and goodness that the world will ever know. Many have chosen to die for their formulated beliefs. The disciplines, outward observances and rituals give concrete expression to an acceptance of Jesus' truth: they are symbolic. And for some of us all these elements of the Christian structure fulfil a need to express devotion, and are a reminder of God as a power independent of us. More than ever before we today acknowledge the effect of mental images on the mind, decision-making and health, especially when intensified by being expressed in action, that is, ritual. Together with theological debate they are, as it were, the household utensils of Christianity.

Yet Jesus rebuked Martha not for doing the household work but for doing it over-solicitously. She missed the essence – and could well have been a little self-important – while Mary went to the point.

Codified Christianity can be accepted only as a support, secondary to motivation. And, being the creation of human intellect and desires, it is highly susceptible to imperfections, to say the least. Ritual can be the beginning of confusion. The contractual small print of Christianity as defined by those in authority through the ages has led to some of the wildest misinterpretations of Jesus and some of the most catastrophic negations of all he stood for when – to borrow Sassoon's words apropos of the First World War – 'the principles of Christianity were either obliterated or falsified for the convenience of all who were engaged in it'. This is especially true when men have enjoyed the temptation to exercise the power that it offers; power of various kinds, political, emotional, worldly, and the dangerous power of self-pride.

For believers and non-believers alike the Church, its teachings and actions, can obscure the truth. It was Teresa of Avila, herself canonized as a saint, who prayed 'from silly devotions and sour-faced saints, Good Lord, deliver us'. Man has always tended to want to depreciate natural wonder, to match the divine to his own stature. Even in music the clever invention of the twelve-note atonal system is based on a destruction of the physical and mathematical laws of harmony and their replacement by an entirely artificial structure, unjustified by nature. Man tends to want to reduce infinity.

Paul himself does not always know when to stop. The element of personality and self in his highly emotional, didactic, often moving and brilliantly analytical excavations into his own awareness of Jesus separate his analyses a long way at times from Jesus' own objective and direct expression. But it must be said that without the early Christian communities that Paul's systematization helped to cohere and without the beginnings of a codified set of beliefs it is unlikely that there would have been any Gospels. And the question must be asked whether the community of believers would continue to exist as a community without rituals and dogma; without them what would be left? It could be that the nonconformist churches, in rejecting some traditional beliefs and rituals, open the way to a livelier faith. Yet they have been more subject to dissension, splinter groups and schism than the mainstream churches.

*   *   *

At its face value the question 'did Jesus intend to create Christianity' means 'did he set out to form a new faith or religion?' Absolutely not. Jesus was born into, brought up in and taught the Jewish faith. He interpreted much of it and presented some of its tenets in a new light. He expanded its dimensions and put life back into some aspects that had become formalities.

This calls for a diversion. In some peculiar way the Jewish perception and practice of religion had undergone a continuous shaping over the centuries. From Jehovah as one of the several divinities worshipped by the tribes, to an anthropomorphic god, to a belief in a single omniscient, omnipresent divine intelligence, there is a sequential pattern of revelation in the Old Testament. This can be said to be unique in world history. Yet some Greek philosophers from the sixth century were feeling their way ever more confidently towards something better than the chaos of the Homeric gods. The Homeric pantheon, in all its venality, intrigue, favouritism, self-seeking, dishonesty and downright comedy, provided the public with the same sort of daily diet of entertainment as the shenanigans of some of today's so-called politicians – the difference lies in the fact that politicians can be lethal. The search pattern runs from Thales and his successors to Xenophanes to Heraclitus, who in the early fifth century before Christ was already describing the Law that created and governs the world as the Logos, the supreme ruler. The cult of Dionysos in particular, prevalent throughout the Eastern Mediterranean and the Near East, served the increasing yearning to transcend the human body and to achieve life after death. But these tendencies were not the same as the focused, continuous and exclusive consciousness of the Jews.

This series of religious insights, especially those of their spiritual leaders called prophets, culminated like an algebraic equation in 'equals Jesus'. It is this thread that the authors of Matthew, Mark and Luke recognized in the unspecific phrase 'as was written in the Scriptures', and demonstrated by John's author in his symbolic alignment of Jesus' sayings and actions with the order of the Jewish religious festivals throughout the year. The composer Sibelius, truly great, introduced a new way of constructing a symphonic movement. He would first reveal fragments of motifs and themes, gradually weave them together with a persistent forward movement and sense of purposeful action and ultimately reveal their origin and meaning in a convincing climactic statement. The parallel with the Bible and Jesus is exact. The more one studies the Old Testament, the more inevitable Jesus' arrival becomes. The corpus of Jewish writings and the detailed rituals of Jewish religious worship and daily routine had by Jesus' time come to represent a highly developed religious awareness and way of life. But the question Jesus posed was, in effect, 'which matters most, the spirit or the letter of the law?'

He wanted to arouse the individual instinct and conscience. He called for the cultivation of the individual's innate alignment with God's spirit. His gift was of a pure, original substance. Righteousness, in the sense of ethical morality, is a man-made concept, however much it is an outward expression of an inner truth. It came as a shock to many of the Jews, blamelessly observing the moral and ceremonial law, that Jesus unreservedly welcomed and loved unrighteous people who came to recognize the spirit that motivated him. The father in the parable of the Prodigal Son runs to throw his arms around his returning son before the son has even apologized.

Jesus the man believed he had a God-given job to do:
but his window of opportunity was finite. So he took
the accepted rituals and systems of Judaism as read. His
intellectual grasp was beyond question; but the intellectual
essence of his message was in any case inherent, while his
appeal had to be as direct, clear and uncomplicated as
possible. It is certain that were he with us today he would
accept much of Christian ritual and dogma, just as he did
with his own Jewish faith. But it is equally certain that his
attitude about what really matters would be the same now
as it was then.

*   *   *

Jesus primarily addressed the individual. But he did intend
to create 'a people of God'. The so-called Sermon on the
Mount declares, in essence, the ethical rules and aims of
a community; the Last Supper, though accounts differ, is
essentially the institution of a community meal; the chosen
number of disciples is symbolic of Israel's twelve tribes. Given
his circumstances and the need to build on what was there
already, for Jesus this 'people of God' meant Israel, with its
history as the people to whom God was revealing himself.
The word 'ecclesia', translated by us as Church, is itself a
translation of a Hebrew word used for the Old Testament
Israel as a people of God. It does not mean a sect or a party
(Jesus firmly refused to lead or start a movement or party)
and it applies to local groups of people as well as the whole.
But he would not have challenged the idea that in its very

strength and nature his message is bound to be universal and cannot be limited to one race. It so happened that the spiritual corpus, the new vision that was his teaching for life, created a religious understanding and philosophy that could be applied, and became available, to men and women everywhere. In this sense, the Jewish people could be said to have fulfilled their self-declared destiny.

Paul knew this; he and the Jewish 'Christian' Church in Jerusalem differed over quite a few points of ritual, observance and policy, since the Jerusalem believers, led by James, found it difficult to think beyond the narrow interpretation of Jesus as the long-expected saviour of Israel. This made Paul's awareness that Jesus' message was all embracing appear to them as almost heretical. But they never differed about the nature, the spirit of Jesus. The differences, discussions and debates that took place in the first-century Church did not obscure or overshadow the message of Jesus. Even so today the Church, in all its many different manifestations and differences, remains a visible expression of a belief in what Jesus represented: it is the community and communities of those who, in their varying ways, degrees and interpretations, accept the message of Jesus as their guide. Such a recognizable entity, however loosely defined, remains a necessity in a material world.

*   *   *

Today the relationship between Jesus' message and the Church to an extent mirrors that between Jesus and the traditional Jewish faith of his day. Jesus revealed a new world for many of his contemporaries. Just as he wanted the then accepted Jewish faith to expand, develop and be fulfilled according to the inspiration and understanding that he brought, so it should be our hope that the Church will be ready to adapt, renew and reinterpret itself in order to bring the spirit that motivated him to the world we now live in.

But one of the differences is that Jesus was speaking to people who had a background of religious practice and identity. The prophet Hosea said 'Israel builds temples and forgets his Maker': but at least there were temples. Particularly among young people today this background hardly, if at all, exists in the West. The computer age has tended to condition the new generation to take a prosaic, prescribed, even unimaginative view of life. The problem is that the further in time from Jesus, the further we are from his direct personal influence. But the Gospels remain: is revelation no longer operative?

The Church cannot afford to cling to ritual that appears no longer valid or credible, or to anthropomorphic dogma, that is, the second coming, the virgin birth, judgement day. The early Church, those who believed in the message of Jesus in the two or three generations after his death, adapted their faith in the light of experience. Indeed, the development itself of a common set of a prescribed beliefs, for example the unfulfilled Second Coming, was an example of striving to preserve but also reinterpret. Surely the modern Church can adapt. Even the Nicene Creed is but a snapshot view of

Christian belief taken at a specific historical point. It can no longer be used as a tool of exclusion, nor should it any longer be allowed to offer a stumbling-block. It is obvious to say that different people need different approaches according to their natures. Some need intellectual structures, some respond to outward expression and observance, some to heightened emotional appeal. All this is offered by the writings of the New Testament.

And the other cornerstone of Christianity, the Lord's Prayer – with its resonances of the age-old Jewish Qaddish prayer, which Jesus illuminates with his own concepts – has a succinct and extraordinary power to speak to us, in its perfect appositeness to the human condition and the limits of our narrow comprehension and capabilities.

Somehow the Church has to make contact with the conscience, the love for that power beyond us, that is instinctive in almost all of us. Jesus did just this: asked which is the first commandment, he replied: 'Love the Lord your God with all your heart, and with all your soul, and with all your mind, and with all your strength: this is the first commandment. And the second is like, love your neighbour as thyself.' His questioner fervently agreed, and added: 'That is far more than all burnt offerings and sacrifices.' And Jesus replied to him, 'You are not far from the Kingdom of Heaven.' The writer of Mark's Gospel emphasizes the finality, satisfaction and completeness of this passage: 'After that nobody ventured to put any more questions to him.'

7

DID JESUS RISE FROM THE DEAD?

The very phraseology of the question is coloured; hazy visual images parade through the mind, of heaven and hell, opening graves, all the symbols of the centuries, especially of the medieval and renaissance imagination. And, with these, come endless theological interpretations and dogma, the concepts of reward and punishment, a misunderstood meaning of faith. Jesus died; his corpse lay in a tomb for about three days; did he then come alive again?

The modern answer is no. That answer is given because we now know that this is a physical impossibility. There may be any one of several reasons for the fact of the empty tomb; and they are irrelevant for anyone searching for spiritual truth. As for the plethora of ingenious solutions offered to invalidate his actual death, they are in reality absurd.

But the contemporary answer would have been 'quite possibly'; at the time it was not as wildly incredible as we now know it to be. Herod quite naturally asked if Jesus was John the Baptist risen from the dead. Other religions of the day celebrated the resurrection of certain of their gods.

Indeed, a resurrection was perhaps the expected mark of a god. It is in the light of this way of thinking that the Resurrection appearances may be seen. How easy or difficult is it to convince oneself, to create an apparent physical reality of a fervently, intensely held train of thought? Did a real live angel appear to Mary to announce the conception of Jesus? Was it an actual voice that spoke to Moses from the bush? What did Joan of Arc really hear? What was the physical reality of Paul's conversion experience? These are all manifestations of various awarenesses of God; in a way there is a certain correspondence with the musician's compulsion to express music, and springing from the same source as music's expressiveness. Is it part of our nature that we have to express the abstract in material, worldly terms?

To believe that Jesus came bodily alive again is wishful thinking. Why wishful? We surely should have advanced beyond needing the reward syndrome; that if we believe in Jesus and try to live life according to his example we will continue our lives into immortality (or, conversely, that we shall be punished after death for bad lives). It is not for that reason we are wishful. Nor, by any stretch of the imagination, can the promise of immortality as a means of getting people to listen to him be ascribed to someone of Jesus' integrity. Jesus' promise of eternal life meant the result of personal alignment with the spirit we call God. Again words can mislead: 'everlasting life' in this sense means being infused with the spirit that is itself infinite and eternal. But he had to express this in human terms and words: his whole life and words were an attempt, like a parable, to illustrate the nature of God in terms that communicate to us. Do we need the promise of immortality as a sort of added-value sales line to encourage us to align ourselves with God? Do we need the Creed as an extended password which allows us access into the system called everlasting life or heaven? Do we still need the threat of hell to persuade us not to behave badly? The concept of hell will seldom, if ever, prevent a determined evil-doer or an impassioned, impetuous action. We can overcome our need to be sustained by a self-centred hope or fear. We can accept that life itself continues eternally and that by embracing the spirit called God, revealed in human terms in Jesus, we identify with eternity.

What then are heaven and hell? Are they words that describe states of the soul, created by the intuitive instinctive conscience? And is this conscience in fact the presence of the Logos – in abundance in some, in paucity in others – within us? Is this what the Bible means in describing us as made in the image of God?

But the concept of the Resurrection is a gorgeous vision, sustaining, cheering, comforting. It is the answer to the threat of evil triumphant; it expresses faith in the indomitable human spirit of optimism; it is a mark of that awareness that distinguishes man from beast. It also is a symbol of our acceptance that there is some barrier between us and God, that we feel a long way from being perfect, that history shows men are not angels. It acknowledges the reality of sin, yet that sin can be overcome: Jesus' crucifixion crucified the failings of our world.

The Resurrection is an image that expresses, again in terms that we can identify with, the wonder of the universe, the joy of life, the eternity of the vital power. It is an allegory of the creative spirit that is infinite, the spirit that physical death cannot destroy, even though as individuals we cease to exist. The body dies: the all-pervading spirit of life is endless. The spirit that was Jesus' is always alive and present.

It was this spirit that was the source of the overwhelming, compelling conviction that Paul, Stephen and all the other believers shared in the traumatic twenty years after Jesus' death, when the vine that Jesus sowed could have withered. They wanted to believe that he had risen from the dead. One of the morals pointed by Chaucer's Magistrate in entertaining his fellow pilgrims is that people tend to believe what they want to believe. It is part of our nature to need company, to feel that we are not totally alone. We even invent an animus for inanimate things, a car, a boat, so that we can share its essence. And for a Christian a living Jesus is a companion: the Resurrection belief is a measure of this need. It was one of the mistakes of the early Church to expect and want Jesus himself to return soon to live with them again; but it was their mistake, not Jesus', and the Church has continued to readjust and reinterpret its initial mistake. Jesus told his disciples that their companion would be the Holy Spirit.

It is a required article of the Christian faith that Jesus went to hell on his death. Hell, according to early Jewish belief, was where one's soul went after physical death: its primary defining feature was as a place separate from God's presence. But the message of the New Testament writings is that nothing can separate us from the love of God, that is, from the primal spirit. This is part of the new revelation. And indeed it remains true even if we accept that physical death is annihilation, since in dying we become part of the universe which is totally infused by the spirit we call God.

The spirit that impelled, we may almost say was, Jesus is alive. But not because of an empty tomb — the Jews of his day conceived body and soul as one entity; therefore an empty tomb was a natural corollary of his triumph; the tomb had to be empty. Not because of Jesus' apparent prophesies of his own resurrection — if any are authentic, they are certainly true in the spiritual sense. The power of the sign of the cross continues to demand a response of some kind, of some degree. Appearing in the written word, in conversation, in art, be the setting religious or secular, be those who witness it believers, atheists or agnostics, it has an effect.

Jesus lives on, through and in the spirit that he embodied. We already, manlike, depreciate the coinage by thinking in terms of a man rising from the dead. Jesus' message is greater than the man; it has its own life, independent of the man. Jesus' death gave wings to his message. His disciples were drawn initially to the personality of Jesus the man; only after his death did the message become paramount. Paul instinctively knew the message was the essence of Jesus: for the writer of John's Gospel, the message was the Logos, the true spirit. Jesus himself knew this: in spite of his only too human 'My God, why have you forsaken me?' he knew that to accept God's will was to share in the spirit of God, the spirit of life itself, and that he was the tool of that spirit. Indeed, how often during the extraordinarily testing circumstances must this centuries' old cry from the Jewish psalms have been echoed by thousands? And yet his spirit continues to live, not least in the extreme experiences of so many of those thousands.

The idea of life after death gives something to live and die for: it may be a false dream, but it is a dream of hope. To envisage something beyond oneself is usefully healthy. Some will argue that a dream is still part of oneself, and that in anticipating life after death one is still living for oneself. If there is no life after death, why attempt to be good, as defined over the centuries and according to any religion? Because – for some reason still as yet to be better defined and explained – man needs to be as good as he can be for his own well-being. Something has to control our lives: it is clear that we do not. We can attempt to, but ours is not the last word. A life without any spark of joy, with no sense of morality, is the life of a psychopath, without the quality of love.

Meanwhile, we are alive. To live means to accept with joy the spirit that impelled Jesus, and that spirit is infinite. Teresa of Avila told us 'Christ has no body now on earth but yours; yours are the only hands with which he can do his work, yours are the only feet.'

And Dylan Thomas knew that we can learn 'to sing in our chains like the sea'.

8

WAS JESUS GOD?

There is an endless multitude of varied aspects to any attempt to discuss this question, historical, metaphysical, doctrinal, instinctive. We know that Jesus never claimed to be God; he never used the phrase Son of God; by implication he denied that he was on a par with God. Repeatedly the accounts show him to have had limited knowledge and to have acknowledged this. It is belief in his message that Jesus emphasizes time and time again. Jesus wanted God to be worshipped, not himself; he wanted peoples' lives to be aligned with the divine power.

He did believe himself – know himself is not too strong a term – to be accredited, commissioned by God, a belief shared not only by his followers but by most of his public at large. It was in this sense that he referred to God as his father; but he emphasized his humanity by using the phrase 'son of man'. The New English Bible rightly translates the comment of the centurion and his men at the foot of the Cross as 'truly this man was a son of God', not 'the son'. His amazing insight into the eternal life power and its application to all aspects of the human condition, to human nature and its capabilities, is described in terms of his being 'sent' by God. It is the Church, from the time of the earliest followers of Jesus right through the various stages of dogma and formalization to today, which has said in effect 'we now know by hindsight that Jesus was God in the form of a man'. This change from Jesus' understanding of himself to that of the Church calls for comment.

In the first place it is a question, as so often, of the viewpoint of Jesus' own day, the accepted norms. People of his day believed in gods, or a god, divine and supernatural beings. They were used to them. In the non-Jewish Greek, Roman and Egyptian world, many of the rulers were worshipped as gods, both in their lifetimes and after their deaths. Even the poet Sophocles was given a shrine – perhaps his contemporaries understood the source of artistic inspiration better than we do. Gods were referred to in anthropomorphic terms without a second thought. To non-Jews the manifest power, authority and inspiration that Jesus embodied might well appear to be that of a god.

The divide between the world of mortals and that of the immortals was not sharply defined. The raw material for the creation of a god was latent in Jesus, that is, in his teaching and recorded actions. The concept of his resurrection, the development of the idea of the virgin birth and the elevation of his remarkable acts of healing into the category of miracles, that is, events defined as something supernatural, are largely due to the then way of thinking: a virgin birth, a resurrection from the dead and the ability to change the natural order of things are the marks of a god, for many in the first century the essential badges of a god. Given contact with the Greek and Roman world, the ensuing metamorphosis of this way of thinking into defined and required dogma was bound to happen. Most of the questions inherent in the elevation of Jesus' status were in due course answered by the theologically elaborated concept of the Trinity.

The Jewish concept of God was something different: the inner sanctuary of the Temple was empty. This means to say that the Jews worshipped an invisible god: unlike any other religions of the day, there were no images. Jesus accepted the received beliefs and traditions of Judaism, and thus provided a link to the concept of a god that was already present in Jewish thought. The revelation that he offered was his innovative application and interpretation, his immense insight into the essential, living meaning of the scriptures; and those that had eyes to see could perceive something in him big enough to save their world. There can be no doubt that his transmutation into a god dates almost immediately from the end of his ministry: some of the first recorded prayers are directed to Jesus.

But there is a much more significant dimension to this discussion. This question presents the most fundamental challenge of all: it involves the nature of what we call God. There have been endless attempts to define God: from Moses, who questioned God and received the short answer 'I am that I am'; to the 'isms' of the eighteenth century – Deism, Pantheism, Theism – and on to Bertrand Russell's ten-year essay in pure mathematics. The account of Moses' experience touches a key element – time, or rather, since time implies something finite, eternity. Just as we cannot comprehend infinite eternity, where the past, present and future exist at once; so we cannot comprehend the infinite space of the universe; so we cannot comprehend that power we call God, the permanent, integral factor in all this. Anything comprehensible is by its very nature a projection of men's minds.

And yet the effort to comprehend and define is sparked off by some sort of innate awareness: conscience is instinctive. Most of us on reflection would agree that somewhere within us is the feeling that we need a god; that is, someone in our own image but beyond human frailties, a role model. There is a whole raft of motivations: men have always tried to create God in their own image, to satisfy their need to worship, to express their inextinguishable optimism, and to soften the sense of their finiteness, their immemorial fear of the unknown, their failure to cope with the acceptance of death and their desire to go on living. In this sense Jesus, with whom we can identify, can serve well as a god. Jesus offers a concrete object of worship: as a human he is easily communicable, while God is a concept less easy to identify with.

Another need generally shared by most of us is the need for companionship. A companion can be a real and physical or an imagined presence. Jesus translates the presence of God into a human personality that, more or less comfortably, we can communicate with, just as Guareschi's Don Camillo talks to the Jesus above his altar. The doctrine of the Resurrection is a measure of this need, and the recorded Resurrection appearances are a manifestation of it.

It is significant that Maeterlinck juxtaposes these threads, in his gem of a book *The Life of the Bee*: 'The discovery of the sign of true intellect outside ourselves procures us something of the emotion Robinson Crusoe felt when he saw the imprint of a human foot on the sandy beach of his island. We seem less solitary than we had believed. . . . We are studying in them [the bees] that which is most precious in our own substance: . . . power of transfiguring blind necessity, of organising, embellishing, and multiplying life . . . of holding in suspense the obstinate force of death'.

Somewhere burning within the human brain is this overwhelming sense of and need for what in John's Gospel is called the Logos, a logical pattern, cause and effect, balance, creative energy, whatever. The concepts defy definition by place, religion, human logic and questioning. Any attempt to define this sense only goes to show the limitations of our human thought processes, the very limitation that a concept of God attempts to transcend.

Our need is one side of the coin. The other side is implicit in God's answer to Moses – 'I am that I am'. This power exists independent of man: that much is clearer today than ever before. It is also in man, as in everything. Jesus' teaching, the message of his life, his personality, come nearest as yet to removing the veil of our limitations and revealing a glimpse of this transcendence. But more – as far as any man has or will ever be, he was this spirit, this power called God, in human form. No wonder that he has always inspired awe and humility; no wonder we men and women have identified him, one of us, with God.

9

WHERE, WHEN AND WHAT DID JESUS EXPECT THE KINGDOM OF GOD TO BE?

How valid today is this concept of the Kingdom of God? What could it possibly mean to the men and women of today's western culture? What actually is it?

Much has been written about the apparent contradictions and ambiguities of Jesus' use of the phrase 'the Kingdom of God (or Heaven)'. It seems that, at least on the surface, his meaning revolved not so much around an intellectual definition as an emotional response. The discussion has particularly focused on whether it meant something immediately realized in the here-and-now or something in the future. If his references are taken at literal face value (and with the assumption that they are all couched in his original words) this is understandable. There was the Jewish hope and expectation that God would inaugurate his Kingdom some time on earth, when all would be well; the fervour of the more specific hope that God would establish Judaea's independence from foreign rule; the interpretation of the messiah as inaugurating this;

and the Jewish identification of themselves as the people of God's Kingdom. Even in Jesus' time there must have been confusion, especially when his words were reported and discussed at second hand by hearsay. And the mistaken anticipation of the Second Coming shared by the early believers also embraced his establishing the Kingdom, a hope that may well have been an invention to sustain their initial frailty in his absence.

'The Kingdom of God is upon you'; 'If I by God's spirit cast out demons, then the Kingdom of God has already come upon you'; 'The tax collectors and the prostitutes will go into the Kingdom of God before you'; 'A rich man will find it hard to enter the Kingdom of God'; to the sensible lawyer, 'You are not far from the Kingdom of God'; asked when would the Kingdom of God come, 'There will be no saying Look here it is or there it is, for in fact the Kingdom of God is among you' (here even the various readings and translations of the Greek for 'among you' reflect some confusion); 'To enter the Kingdom of Heaven you must become like a child'; 'Your Kingdom come'; 'Set your mind on his Kingdom and all the rest will come to you'; thus Jesus' direct references, and more. He uses similes and metaphors in his parables to help to describe the Kingdom, seed, yeast, a fishing net, a wedding feast, a vineyard, a fig tree, investment finance, a hidden treasure, a pearl of great price; and more.

The Aramaic word used by Jesus that is translated in the Gospels by the Greek *basileia*, Kingdom, in fact means the rule of God, or God's spirit in action. The here-and-now aspect was correct in that embracing Jesus' message offered a new inspiration and the chance of aligning oneself with God's spirit, the Logos as John's Gospel calls it (the law of God in action). It was not correct in that Jesus was not inaugurating, or would not inaugurate by his Second Coming, a sort of immediate heaven, a utopia. Such a puerile view belittles the depth of Jesus' understanding, his very considerable realism and his knowledge of human nature. He took care to demonstrate and state that he did not see himself as inaugurating any sort of earthly Kingdom. It was only with reluctance at the end of his ministry that he revealed his assessment of himself as the messiah, God's messenger; and then it was as a messiah very different from general public expectation. To accept this utopian idea would be to allow the inevitable needs and scope of man's own limited and immediate vision to warp Jesus' message. Nevertheless, Jesus used the concept to emphasize urgency as an essential spur to wake people up; his time was limited.

It is a moot point whether Jesus' understanding of his mission to usher in the Kingdom deepened during his active ministry or whether it had matured, of knowing purpose or unconsciously, over the years of preparation before his 'going public'. There is also the question how far his personal experiences shaped his thinking. Certainly in music, and possibly in other arts, the events and circumstances of a composer's life had no direct correlation with the character and emotion of the work he produced, until the Romantic era of the nineteenth century, foreshadowed by Mozart's Requiem (and to a lesser extent his Masonic Funeral Music). In dire health and with grave monetary difficulties

— whatever the cause of the latter may have been — Mozart wrote supremely joyful and confident music. There is no direct link at all between personal drama and the work of art. But there is a link, in that, again to take Mozart as a case study, as he grew older, from childhood to manhood, his inspiration approached closer and closer to the nature of the spirit that impelled him. The depth of emotional communication, of wonder, and of insight increases. At times the revelation, indescribable in words, becomes complete. Thus it may have been with Jesus.

On balance, the references to the Kingdom deal more with something already going on, expanding, growing, developing. Jesus is the sower of the seed. He was himself under God's rule, already in God's Kingdom and a concrete manifestation of it. Therefore one's entry into it, to join in the feast, depended on one's attitude to Jesus. Paul recognized this: 'If anyone is in Christ there is a new creation.' Jesus demonstrates the spirit that will predicate the future along the right lines, both for the individual's personal future and that of society as the people of God. It is an uncomfortably obvious truism that, if most of us tried, each according to his or her own nature and ability, to understand the spirit that created Jesus' message and allow it to work in us, the world would become a better place. There would be a renewal, a rebirth of the world in line with God's spirit. But, again, the Kingdom is not something we create, a sort of utopia: it exists for us to enter. God reigns, to use anthropomorphic terms again, eternally; but Jesus is the chance offered to accept his rule.

It was this fact that underlay the hostility of the Jewish Establishment, led by Caiaphas. Jesus accepted the Jewish Law; but he called for a response not to the Law but to the spirit that manifested itself in him. And that spirit was the source of man's search to create the Law. In this sense he replaced the Law without destroying it; he made sense of it. But the Law, which threatened to become an end in itself, was not the Kingdom. 'Until John the Baptist there were the Law and the Prophets; since then there is the good news of the Kingdom of God.' The real truth behind the Law was at hand in the next stage of revelation, embodied in and by Jesus, a revelation for which John's Gospel helps to draw back the curtain. Perhaps there is a further corollary: you do not have to be a Jew to believe in Jesus; you do not have to be a 'Christian' as currently defined by the Church (in its various manifestations) to believe in Jesus' message. The Church is but a flawed human effort to manifest, in one way, the Kingdom of God on earth. To order the purposes of one's life in accordance with the spirit that impelled Jesus is already in some manner to participate in the Kingdom of Heaven, when life embraces another dimension. Blake put it in another, highly graphic way: 'What it will be Questioned When the Sun rises do you not see a round Disk of fire somewhat like a Guinea O no no I see an Innumerable company of the Heavenly host crying Holy Holy Holy is the Lord God Almighty.'

It remains for the writer of John's Gospel to put his finger on the crucial point (Mark also does this once in quoting what Jesus may actually himself have said). The spirit called

God is the spirit of life. The writer uses the word 'life' throughout as synonymous with the other Gospel writers' 'Kingdom of God'. Responding to Jesus, recognizing and rejoicing in the spirit called God is to enter the Kingdom of Heaven. The primal force is king. If we accept that there is the primal force – the force that the writers of Genesis had already recognized and attempted to describe – the Logos, then Jesus' sayings about the Kingdom hang together as the way to life, of infinitely more significance than our own mortal and finite nature. Nor, seen in this light, does death loom so large.

10

THE TENTH QUESTION

Several strong characters, at first glance a most unlikely company, have found their way into these pages, in spite of my promised efforts: Oscar Wilde, Teresa of Avila, Dylan Thomas, Giuseppe di Lampedusa, William Blake, FitzGerald's Omar Khayyam, W. H. Auden, Alexander Solzhenitsyn, Guareschi's Don Camillo, Munch, Mark Twain and Maeterlinck; even Mozart and Sibelius have made a brief appearance. What would they choose to make their tenth question, each according to their nature and their historic period? But it is now the turn of the reader to ask — and perhaps answer — his or her own question.

First, to replay the themes: then, to offer some questions as to the main theme of the next movement.

*　　*　　*

Reason, ethics, an awareness of beauty, a sense of right and wrong in all categories of their manifestation, logic, scientific rules and reactions, rhythms, balance — the list of examples can be made by each one of us according to experience — all these are the outward evidence of a power

innate in the world. It permeates all; it is evident in a
myriad ways, with new ones always appearing.

This power appears, in the ultimate resolution, to be
indefinable. It has been given many names, the soul of the
world, the Holy Spirit, the Logos, and many, many more.
God is probably the most frequently used name for that
power cable whose interwoven strands go to make up
the energy of the world. But finite words cannot describe
something that is timeless and absolute. Words destroy
the medium. Words use anthropomorphic terms: such
terms can mislead and have misled our understanding –
in some instances they have caused false structures to be
built; but they are unavoidable. Words and translations
have caused as much confusion as clarity; but they are one
of our essential means of communication with each other
– the other means involve the senses and therefore the
arts. It is crucial we recognize that the power has always
been described in terms related to the then knowledge
and experience of each succeeding age. What name or title
is used is of no great significance as long as this power is
recognized.

Here is the right place for a digression that helps to define
further some of the implications of the word Logos. It is not
really a mystical and esoteric word. It is the Septuagint's
Greek translation of wisdom, as defined in Proverbs 8.
Philo, the Jewish philosopher of Alexandria, discusses it,
probably some years before Jesus' death. To him, the Word,
the Logos, stands between the Creator and the created,
partaking of both elements.

Spiritual concepts and emotions are impossible to communicate fully by words alone. It is for this reason that music means more to us than words; it can produce a frisson of indefinable insight. It serves as a bridge of transcendency between our awareness, however instinctive, acknowledged or not, of the Logos, and our human condition. In the same way, Jesus, a physical presence, is such a bridge.

We lead two lives – the inner life of the thoughts, pictures, emotions that continuously throng our heads, both conscious and unconscious, produced usually without our will; and the outward life, the words (already a debased medium of expression), gestures and images that we, like actors, choose of our own will to express to others. Jesus would seem to have integrated these two lives, by living out naturally and easily his convictions, and giving concrete expression, without conscious planning, to the spirit that motivates him.

Philo's idea was not new. It is adumbrated in the Old Testament, specifically in Numbers 16. And, indeed, it makes sense that a human being such as Jesus should embody to an extraordinary degree the innate sense of order, cause and effect, balance and harmony – a sense that guides us, for all our mortal and flawed natures, from leading mankind over the precipice edge. And so the circle is joined with the idea that conscience is instinctive.

But the power, the Logos, is also independent of us. As the Jewish authors of Genesis said, we are made in God's image; and that means that God is not made in ours. To the question 'Which is the Potter, pray, and which the Pot?'

the Book of Job answers very clearly: 'Where were you when I created the world?' As Solzhenitsyn pointed out, 'Man, who has declared himself to be the centre of existence in this world, has been unable to create a balanced spiritual system.' This is a difficult thought to grapple with, and may be the reason for man's invention of the negative concept of fearing God. But it is true that once we come to believe we are the last word, we have lost awareness of the Logos.

The man Jesus embodied this power, this essence: this it was that impelled his mind, gave him his insight and illuminated his decisions. In terms of the human condition, his life, teaching and very nature are the best demonstration of this power yet seen. And even if you tend to believe that God is, after all, a human projection of aspects of man's nature, how superbly do the message and life of Jesus vindicate the best in man, the channelling of this element, divine or not, in us. Again, Solzhenitsyn: 'a genuine artistic work is irrefutably convincing and carries its proof within itself. Works which have drawn on truth and presented it to us in a live, concentrated form, grip us and communicate themselves to us compellingly. Nobody, even centuries later, will ever be able to refute them.' Again to revert to the nature of music, in W. H. Auden's poem 'The Composer': 'All the others translate: ... /Only your song is an absolute gift /You alone .../Are unable to say an existence is wrong, / And pour out your forgiveness like a wine.' Such is Jesus' witness.

The New Testament expresses the concept in different ways. Jesus said 'the Kingdom of God is come upon you'; Paul, 'If any man is in Christ there is a new creation'; John,

'The Logos became flesh and dwelt among us.' There was a common conviction that (to use anthropomorphic terms again) God, through Jesus as messenger, had offered us an opportunity to align ourselves with his spirit. This was the revelation of the New Testament. But the revelation must now continue: it cannot stop with an attitude which in many ways is still that of the first century.

*   *   *

Because of the infinite nature of the power that made Jesus behave, think, act and speak as he did it is only to be expected that human intellect will have found meanings of endless depth in his actions and words; and, given man's needs and inventiveness, that such meanings should have been formulated into theological and social structures. Everything that Jesus is reported to have said – everything that carries some element of authenticity and is not clearly or obviously a reflection of belief, ritual or interpretation of the time when it was written down or added to – has a deeper meaning than the practical mind of man is inclined to give it. The true meaning and impact of his mission lie behind its events and sayings, which are indications, signposts, produced as outward signs of the inner spirit. As such they have a unity; they express – are the outcome of – a single power. There is little or no dividing line in the Gospels between fact and allegory. This is what so many fail to see or to accept. This is why Jesus was, has been and is misunderstood.

It does not matter whether Jesus rose bodily and materially from the dead; it does not matter whether he was conceived by a virgin. It is enough to accept and rejoice in loving this power, through understanding Jesus. Aligning oneself with the nature of Jesus, with what he revealed, enables us to experience this spirit in our own lives. This recognition, this acceptance, this love is the conduit for the primal power. This alignment may be emotional, intellectual, rational, according to the nature and capability of each of us. The sense of love that is in most, if not all, of us is the key element and starting point. The result will be positive and creative in one way or another: the power will manifest itself.

*   *   *

If this power is so all-pervasive, why do we need the Church, its structures, its codifications and disciplines? A partial answer lies in another question: why does a musician have to toil hourly for years in order to be able to play an instrument? Why does an artist have to study, develop and experiment with technique in order to be able to express something visually? Why does an athlete have to train? The Church, as a tangible expression of Jesus' teachings, is a necessity in a material world.

It must be allowed that codified Christianity is a two-edged sword: negative in the hands of the religious power-brokers, positive as a bulwark against Caesar, the secular state subject only to man's whims and desires. It is a structure that protects the integrity of man's conscience. At least in part, this is what Sir Thomas More's stand against Henry VIII was about, not the narrow-minded obstinacy of a proud conservative. Codified Christianity has always threatened the wished-for absolutism of temporal power. Such a sword is as essential now as ever, and more so.

But, in general terms, the Church appears now to be stagnating and fragmenting just as was the Jewish traditional religion in Jesus' day. There seems to be a decline in the ability of the organized Church to communicate. Is this due to loss of contact with Jesus — are we too far removed from his life? Or too reliant on replacing him with ritual? Or too insistent on no longer admissible beliefs? There is now no central, cohesive, continual revelation pressing us forward, such as shines through the Old Testament: nor is there someone, an acknowledged presence, to focus and define this revelation and to carry it on.

Jesus, in his day incredibly innovative, called for a response. The response in turn called for action. What action is called for now? Do we need a spring-clean of Christianity, so that the Church may concentrate on the spirit of Jesus? Is there still a chance for the Church? So far these essays have been an attempt to share thoughts. But thoughts can, and often should, lead to action. In these essays there has been an underlying pulse. No domain of thought or expression remains static — science, music, art, religion, law. The laws, that is the ritual and the dogma of a religious faith, are no exception. And these laws must adapt and develop or be broken, in whole or in part. Has the time arrived for another breakthrough, another revelation? Why should the Church not now adapt and refresh itself, as did the early Church? Is this possible? Have we all reached the necessary maturity? What of the children of today, who in so many schools go without spiritual teaching, whose minds are not open to awe? Is there a need to formulate yet another accepted Creed, to create an alternative set of rituals? Can what is already good in the Church be used? Will our priests speak out and act meaningfully from their hearts, of joy? Does it matter what you believe, or how you see the question of religion, as long as you get the fundamental message that to love God is the key to the Kingdom of God, and allow this love to guide you, without resorting to man-made images and concepts? I am not positing a doctrine of faith without works – in the sense that, as long as you have faith (how defined, one asks), it doesn't matter what you achieve. If the spirit that impelled Jesus is experienced in us, is allowed to impel us, then works – actions, achievements, attitudes – will follow.

Jesus appeared incredibly innovative when he relegated the central significance of the Temple at Jerusalem, replacing its concrete and symbolic dominance by life unified with God through worship of and adherence to the Logos. Indeed this was so shocking to some of his contemporaries that they felt that they had to seek his death. Our own religious buildings, our churches and cathedrals, are inspiring witnesses to the faith and dedication of their creators in their day, and can touch the hearts, with very few exceptions, of the most ardent atheists. They may still arouse wonder and a sense of the continuity of Christianity. But to many they have become a barrier to experiencing the joy of life.

Yet traditional images and concepts can be extremely effective. If we accept and use them, with the reservation that they are only adumbrations of the primal spirit, reflections in the human mirror, allegories, attempts at explanation, then they can become valuable symbols and a means of communicating truths and principles and offering the strength of companionship. There have been times when Islam, Judaism and Christianity have coexisted amicably, in communities, countries and the world at large. They have shared spiritual experience and thought as well as scientific and philosophical knowledge, both knowingly and by symbiosis; and yet each respected the other's independence and modes of approach and expression. This was because of an acknowledgment that each has a common awareness of the same God, in the sense of an ultimate spirit and source of life. Can an open recognition of this spirit lead to a revival and development of this positive ethos? Once this attitude is acknowledged, there is a chance for today's world that interest in and practice of Jesus' message will revive. Who has the courage to lead the way? Who must introduce the new reformation? What shape will it take?

*   *   *

To study Jesus is, for me, to develop an increasing awareness of something always known. Yes, I have run the risk of prattling about God; I am a dilettante in theological matters. Yet something has led me, butterfly-like, to explore many blossoms along the way. And so I will add one more to that unlikely company who have found their way into these pages, Carmen de Gasztold of the Abbaye at Limon-par-Igny, by quoting from her Prayer of the Butterfly, 'Where was I? Oh yes! Lord, I had something to tell you: Amen.'

THANKS

This book's existence is thanks to more than a few people, friends, acquaintances, experts, through the years. It is something of a personal confession, and so I will mention only some who have become part of my life. Tom Pasteur, formerly Deputy Chairman of Faber and Faber, persuaded me that it had some worth: 'I am sure that you should publish it,' and explained why. His detailed comments have been woven in. The lively intellect of Dr Brian Priestman, international conductor and a man of wide horizons, has challenged me from the interesting viewpoint of an unbeliever from a famous Quaker family. Rabbi Malcolm Weisman's encouragingly positive and often very direct comments as we met in the course of my professional work have stood me in good stead. He caused me to rethink particularly Question 1. Michael Polkinghorne's kindness and generosity showed me how thought leads to action and helped me to see what many non-Christians are looking for. And I thank the late Ron Bambury, one-time vicar of St Augustine's, Cashmere, New Zealand, who started me on this road.

As for expert authors, I am much indebted to *Jesus*, by A. N. Wilson; *The Authentic Gospel of Jesus*, by Geza Vermes; *Jesus: The Evidence*, by Ian Wilson; E. P. Sanders' *The Historical Figure of Jesus*; and A. M. Hunter's *The Unity of the New Testament*. All these are closely argued major works, each a synthesis of far-reaching research and analysis.

At all stages my wife Elizabeth has been there. Music communicates directly, and so it can be in love and marriage: words about music or marriage are dangerous, debasing meaning and limiting expression. The least I can say is that her patience, handling of practical issues, skills as an editor, faith, very objective criticism, all and more have played an essential part. And, finally, the book took shape in a holiday discussion over a splendid tête-à-tête supper in the ancient Spanish village of Perelada, not far from Dalí's home. I hope the book truly reflects all these elements.